China

Through The Eyes of An American University President

眼中的中國 一位美国校长

Author:Sidney A. McPhee (U.S.A)

西德尼·A·麦克菲（美）著

Translator: Zhang Xiaoge

张晓舸 译

湖南美术出版社

China Acknowledgements 致谢

Few worthwhile endeavors are ever truly accomplished alone. This book is no exception. I owe a great deal of thanks to a number of friends and colleagues, both in the United States and China, who played an important role in helping to make this publication of my photographic work a reality.

Special thanks to:
Dr. Guanping Zheng, Professor and Director of the Confucius Institute, Middle Tennessee State University, Murfreesboro, Tennessee (USA), for his advice, support and cultural insight throughout the development of this book.

Dr. Dong Renjie, Professor and Director of International Office, China Agricultural University，Beijing, China, for introducing me to China by arranging and coordinating many of my opportunities to photograph various cities and locations, and for being a very good personal friend.

Officials at Hanban (Confucius Institute Headquarters), Beijing, China, for their generosity in sponsoring this book. I wish to especially acknowledge Dr. Xu Lin, Director-General of Hanban, General Director of the Confucius Institute Headquarters; Wang Yongli, Deputy Director General, Confucius Institute Headquarters; and Shen Tian, Coordinator, Confucius Institute Affairs, Confucius Institute Headquarters, for their support of this creative effort.

Dr. Chen Zhangliang, Vice Governor of Guangxi Zhuang Autonomous Region, and former President of China Agricultural University, for his great kindness, support and for being my good "Chinese brother".

Dr. Yang Huixing, Secretary General, Guangxi Association of Overseas and Returned Scholars, Nanning, China, for her support.

Thanks China South Publishing & Media Group and Hunan Fine Arts Publishing House for the publication of this book.

I would also like to thank the following senior chinese university officials and leaders for their friendship and support in coordinating opportunities for me to see the best of China: Cui Pengfei, Chairman of University Council and Director of University Administration Committee, Hangzhou Normal University, Hangzhou, China; Dr. Ye Gaoxiang, President and Vice Chancellor, Hangzhou Normal University, Hangzhou, China; Professor Qu Zhenyuan, Chairman, University Council, China Agricultural University, Beijing, China; Dr. Ke Bingsheng, President, China Agricultural University, Beijing, China; Dr. Lin Zhengfan, former President, Hangzhou Normal University, Hangzhou, China; Dr. Wang Limin, former President, Northwest Normal University, Lanzhou, China; and Sun Xuewu, former President, Northwest Agriculture and Forestry University, Shanxi, China.

Additional thanks should be extended to several other individuals from various universities, who assisted me during my many visits to China over the years:

Hangzhou Normal University (Hangzhou, China): Mrs. Zhou Lan, Ms Zhushu

Xia,office of International Cooperative and Exchange; Mr. Hu Genqing, Former Director of the International Office of HNU.

China Agricultural University (Beijing, China): Zhang Wenli, Vice President; Mr. Liu Ran, Office of International Relations; Yin Tang, Deputy Chief of Division for Cooperation & Exchange Programs; Ms. Tang Ying, Chief, International Cooperation in American and Oceanic Region Office of International Relations; Wang Dapeng, Driver; Liu Xiao, former student of CAU and current student of MTSU; and Liu Tong, former student of CAU and current student of University of Maryland.

Hunan Normal University (Changsha, Hunan, China): Dr. Jiang Hongxin, Vice President; Tang Jianwen, Director, Office of International Exchange and Cooperation; and Tang Cunzhong, Deputy Director, Office of International Exchange and Cooperation.

Northwest Normal University (Lanzhou, China): Professor Quan Xiaohui, Director of the Office of International Cooperation and Exchange Division; Mr. Yang Guoke, Executive Assistant, Office of International Cooperation and Exchange Division; and Mr. Hu Wencheng, Executive Assistant, Office of International Cooperation and Exchange.

Northwest Agriculture and Forestry University (Shanxi, China): Luo Jun, Director of the Office of International Relations.

Central South University of Forestry and Technology (Changsha, Hunan, China): Dr. Yuan Guangming, Vice Director, International Office and Wang Jianxia, Director, Office of Alumni Relations, Central South University of Forestry and Technology.

Additionally, I owe considerable thanks to Dr. Tonjanita Johnson for her hard work in the development of the narrative components of this book. I was extremely fortunate to have Dr. Johnson with her vast professional, creative and technical expertise working with me to make this book a reality.

I also want to thank Kimberly Edgar, my long-time and trusted Executive Assistant, for her professional loyalty and assistance with this project and so many others over the years.

I would also like to express my love and appreciation to my wife, Liz, and my children, Sidney Anthony and Seneca. Through my travels and their own personal experiences, they, too, have come to love and appreciate the Chinese people and culture.

Finally, I want to extend a few sincere words of gratitude to the people of China and to those whose photographs appear within this book. Thank you for being outstanding ambassadors for your great country and for giving me the honor and privilege of showcasing your beauty and warmth for the entire world to see.

人终其一生几乎没有一件事能单凭一己之力达成，本书也不例外。在此，我首先要感谢众多朋友和诸位同事，无论他们身在美国还是中国。没有他们的鼎力相助，我的摄影作品难以结集出版。

我要特别感谢：

郑冠平博士，现任美国田纳西州默弗里斯伯勒中田纳西州州立大学孔子学院主任及教授。感谢他在本书撰写过程中提出的宝贵意见，给予的不懈支持和独到深邃的文化见解。

董仁杰博士，现任中国北京中国农业大学国际合作与交流处处长及教授。感谢他精心安排行程、协调各方关系，使我有机会拍摄中国多个城市及文化景点。他与我私交甚密，能拥有这样一位挚友我倍感荣幸。

中国北京国家汉办（孔子学院总部）各级官员，感谢他们对本书的大力赞助。借此机会，我想特别感谢国家汉办主任、孔子学院总部总干事许琳博士，国家汉办副主任、孔子学院总部副总干事王永利先生以及孔子学院总部孔子学院事务协调员申田。因为他们的支持，才有了这极富创造性的工作结晶。

陈章良博士，曾任中国广西中国农业大学校长，现任广西壮族自治区副主席。陈博士为人和善，积极支持我的工作，是我在中国的"好哥们"。

杨慧星博士，现任中国南宁广西欧美同学会秘书长，感谢她的大力支持。

感谢中南出版传媒集团和湖南美术出版社出版此书。

我还要感谢以下大学的中方领导，他们的友谊和多方协调使我有幸欣赏到中国最美的一面。他们是：中国杭州师范大学校党委书记崔鹏飞、校长和副书记叶高翔博士、前任校长林正范先生，中国北京中国农业大学党委书记瞿振元教授、校长柯炳生博士，中国兰州西北师范大学前校长王利民博士以及中国陕西咸阳西北农林科技大学前校长孙学武先生。

此外，我还要感谢这些年来在我多次访问中国期间给予我协助与支持的各位同仁，他们是：

中国杭州师范大学国际合作与交流处前工作人员柯丽亚、吴晓伟、陈辰、周兰女士、夏祝淑女士以及前任处长徐根清先生。

中国北京中国农业大学校长助理张文丽，国际关系科刘冉先生，交流合作计划科印瑭先生，美洲及大洋洲国际合作与关系科科长唐莹女士，司机王大鹏，前中国农业大学、现中田纳西州立大学学生刘宵，前中国农业大学、现马里兰州立大学学生刘彤。

中国湖南长沙湖南师范大学副校长蒋洪新，国际交流合作处处长唐建文以及国际交流合作处副处长唐存忠。

中国兰州西北师范大学国际合作交流处处长权晓辉教授，国际合作交流处行政助理杨国科先生以及国际合作交流处行政助理胡文成先生。

中国陕西咸阳西北农林科技大学国际交流与合作处处长罗军。

中国湖南长沙中南林业科技大学国际合作与交流处副处长袁光明博士以及校友关系办公室主任王建峡。

此外，我还要感谢托詹妮塔·L·约翰逊博士对本书文稿所做的辛勤工作。

我还要感谢金柏利·埃德加女士，谢谢她对这个项目的大力支持。非常幸运，能与这些业务娴熟并极富创新意识的技术专家一道工作，有了他们的支持本书才能最终付梓。

我还要感谢我的妻子莉丝及我可爱的孩子西德尼·安东尼和塞内卡。正是他们对我的爱以及对我工作的理解与支持使我的工作得以顺利进行。通过我旅行的所见所闻以及他们自己的亲身体验，他们已经喜爱并懂得欣赏中国人民和中国文化的美。

最后，我想向中国人民以及那些出现在本书照片中的人表示衷心的感激。谢谢你们充当贵国杰出的文化大使，使我有机会向全世界展示你们的迷人风采与热情好客。

SMALL LENS, BIG VISION

小镜头中的大视野

I became acquainted with Dr. Sidney A. McPhee, president of Middle Tennessee State University (MTSU), when the university was applying for the establishment of a Confucius Institute. Though we only met on a few occasions, we soon became dear friends. I was deeply impressed by his humorous wisdom, his strategic foresight, his international vision, and also his polite, scholarly manners.

As a renowned expert on higher education, Dr. McPhee has taken leadership positions at many prestigious universities in the United States. Since he took the position as the tenth president of MTSU in 2001, he has led the university to continuous and substantial progress. In 2011, MTSU was elevated to Comprehensive/Doctoral status by the Carnegie Corp., one of the nation's oldest, and most influential foundations.

Dr. McPhee has long advocated for China-US People-to-People Exchange in culture and education, which have yielded great results. Under his advocacy, MTSU established cooperative partnerships with many Chinese universities, including China Agricultural University, Northwest Normal University in Lanzhou, Hangzhou Normal University and Hunan Normal University among others. He has personally overseen the establishment and development of the Confucius Institute in MTSU which, with efforts from both sides, has grown to be a center of Chinese language teaching and bilateral cultural exchanges for the state of Tennessee.

Dr. McPhee has deep feelings for China, and has visited China many times. He has been to many places in China, from famous mountains to beautiful

我是在中田纳西州州立大学孔子学院申办过程中，与西德尼·A·麦克菲校长（Sidney A. McPhee）结识的。虽然仅有几次接触，但我们很快就成了好朋友。他睿智幽默，富有战略远见和国际化理念，彬彬有礼，风采既儒雅又昂扬。

麦克菲先生是一位著名的高等教育专家，曾在美国多所著名大学担任管理职务。2001年出任中田纳西州州立大学校长以来，带领这所大学不断进取，取得了长足进步，2011年被卡纳基基金会认定为"综合性/授予博士学位大学"。

麦克菲先生积极倡导中美人文交流，在中美教育文化交流方面倾注了大量心血，作出了很大贡献。在他的积极推动下，中田纳西州州立大学与中国农业大学、兰州西北师范大学、杭州师范大学、湖南师范大学等数所中国大学建立了合作关系。他亲自领导了中田纳西州州立大学孔子学院的建设和发展，在中美双方的共同努力下，孔子学院的汉语教学和文化交流活动开展得有声有色，已经成为田纳西州的汉语教学和中美文化交流中心。

麦克菲先生对中国怀有深厚的感情，曾经多次来中国访问，游历名山大川和城市乡村，足迹遍布中国大江南北。他认为中国是一个辽阔美丽、充满迷人魅力的国度，亲自拍摄了大量摄影作品。《一位美国大学校长眼中的中国》精选了两百张他亲手拍摄的照片。光影交错中，既有对中国自然风光和传统文化的捕捉，也有对普通中国人喜怒哀乐的真实写照，他用镜头语言解读着中国自然文化多样性和博大精深的文化传统，以独特的视角热情赞美了一个正在崛起、大踏步融入世界的东方国家的风采。每幅或

rivers, and from urban cities to rural areas. He regards China as a beautiful and enchanting country with abundant resources. He has personally captured the many aspects of Chinese charm through his extensive photographic works. This photo album: China through the eyes of an American university president collects 200 photos shot by Dr. McPhee himself. Through a play of light and shadow, Dr. McPhee has not only captured natural sceneries and traditional Chinese culture, but also vividly depicted the everyday life of Chinese people. Through his lens, Dr. McPhee is interpreting the diversity of Chinese nature, and the richness of traditional culture. From a unique perspective, China's rise and integration into the world arena is been vividly depicted and acclaimed. Each single or category of photo is complemented with a brief introduction or comments from the photographer, along with famous quotes from the great Chinese thinker Confucius. Using the photos and the stories behind; Dr. McPhee introduces the real China to his American and world audience, and shares with them his joy and happiness.

It was with a strong sense of curiosity that I started to look through the photo album of Dr. McPhee. I was deeply conquered by his unique personality, and moved by his deep passion for China. I would love to recommend this album to readers all over the world. I assure that you will embark on a unique journey into traditional and modern China, and personally experience its passion, its vigor and its many charms.

Xu Lin
Director General of HANBAN
Chief Executive of Confucius Institute Headquarters

同类照片均配简短文字介绍及摄影者感言，并配以相关的孔子箴言。麦克菲先生希望通过这些照片及照片背后的故事，与中外读者分享他的快乐和喜悦，告诉美国以及世界人民中国的真实模样。

我抱着浓厚的兴趣拜读了麦克菲先生的这部摄影集，深为麦克菲先生独特的个人魅力所折服，也深为他对中国发自内心的深情厚意而感动。所以，我非常愿意向中外读者推荐这本摄影集，我想读者一定能够从中感受到中国传统与现代交融、活力与激情并发的多彩魅力。

许琳
国家汉办主任
孔子学院总部总干事

*The journey of a thousand miles begins with
a single step!*
— Laozi

千里之行，始于足下。

——老子

China:

THROUGH THE EYES
OF AN AMERICAN
UNIVERSITY PRESIDENT

魅力 中國
一位美国大学校长眼中的中国

Sheer enjoyment and the opportunity to be proud of one's work are often the highest intended consequences for individuals who invest their time and resources in hobbies and other projects of leisure. Having others acknowledge the splendor or greatness of what results from one's extracurricular passion is a rare joy for most amateurs and is generally received with much surprise when such a rarity occurs. Such is the case with my photography and the recent interest that so many people around the world have expressed about the images of China that I have taken as a recreational photographer.

Having spent more than three decades in the fast-paced, ever-changing field of higher education, photography has been a true source of enjoyment and escape for me for many years. I feel extremely fortunate to live at time when the opportunities to experience life in other cultures and to capture the essence of those experiences through photography are more widely available than ever before. Unlike most true amateur photographers, I have had the good fortune of being able to go beyond simply snapping nice photos of interesting places. I have been able to develop unusually deep connections with the places and subjects of my work, which has resulted in a surprising appreciation of my artistic efforts by others.

While I am both flattered and humbled by the support that I have received in the publication of this work, I must admit that a book was never the goal of my efforts. The photographs included in this book reflect only a small glimpse into a very exciting journey that started out of my simple intrigue of a very complex nation. Yet, I am excited about this opportunity to share my work with a larger audience and remain fully convinced that it presents a vital and worthwhile message of beauty, diversity, growth and

有闲情雅趣并乐此不疲，为它倾注再多的时间与精力也无怨无悔，以至终有所成。回望自己的劳动成果，谁又能不欣欣然而为之洋洋自得呢？但是，对于大多数如我一样的业余爱好者来说，纵有满腔热情，若要他人夸赞其作品魅力无穷、大气宏伟也实非易事。一旦真有这样的奇迹发生，其惊喜之情真是难于言表。我的摄影爱好正是如此。近年来，世界各地掀起一股中国印象热，我亦不能免俗，也将镜头对准了中国这个古老的国度。

在飞速发展、日新月异的高等教育领域，我已辛勤耕耘三十余载，摄影成为我消遣娱乐的主要方式和真正的快乐之源。有幸生活在文化交流与科学技术日益发展的今天，使我不仅有机会体验异国他乡的风土人情，更能借助摄影技术捕捉异域文化的精髓。每到一处风景名胜，多数业余摄影爱好者都是走马观花，拍几张照片就匆匆离开。我得工作之便，于每一处风景名胜均能驻足观赏、细细品味其间的奥妙，在摄影作品与拍摄地之间建立起一种非比寻常的联系，这也正是我的摄影作品受人称道的原因。

得知此书即将出版，我甚是欣喜，又甚感惶恐。必须承认，出书从来不是我工作的最终目的。本书包含的摄影作品不过是那些激动人心的旅程的冰山一角，借以撩开中国这个神秘国度的面纱。当然，有机会与广大的读者朋友分享我的工作成果确实是一件非常愉悦的事。我相信，本书会向那些用心领会书中美景的读者传递一条重要而有价值的信息，那就是中国的美丽、多姿、成长与蜕变。有一点要提请大家注意，虽然本书展现的是中国最美好的一面，但这并不意味着我对它的缺点、政治议题及社会问题视而不见，只是对此我选择的是让其他作者来言说。

transformation for those who take the time to explore its content. I think that it is important to note that while this work presents the best of what China has become, I am in no way oblivious to the fact that, like other countries, it has its share of warts, political issues and social concerns. However, I have chosen to leave those things to someone else's book.

The photographic work featured within these pages reflects over 10 years of travel to more than 60 cities and towns throughout China. The photos speak to the ever-increasing interest and curiosity of individuals from America and around the world to know more about China as an emerging world power and to get a glimpse into what the country is really like from the perspective of an American university president, who has and continues to build professional and personal relationships with institutions and individuals across China and actively promotes increased cultural understanding of this intriguing country.

Like other organizational leaders, university presidents often have the responsibility of seeing things from a view of "30,000 feet". From this perspective, we are able to observe the beauty of how people and processes work together and develop impressions about the world that help shape our thoughts and our approach to leadership. The challenge that we often face when viewing the world from such a high vantage point is how to capture and communicate those impressions in a manner which celebrates, motivates and activates those who are on the ground. The purpose of this book is to do just that—to utilize pictures to celebrate China's history and all that it has become; to motivate readers to want to know more about China, its culture and its people; and to spur individuals to action as it relates to visiting China so that they may develop their own impressions about this dynamic world power that is having an ever-increasing impact on everything from the world economy to its educational and social culture.

Without a doubt, China is a very interesting country, primarily because of its diversity...There really is no one China. The differences in people and the topography make it a very unique place. On top of that, it is a land marked by tremendous history and culture. As I noted previously, this book is symbolic of my own personal journey, one that has taken me down unforgettable pathways of new perspectives, greater knowledge and understanding, and, most importantly, unimaginable experiences and friendships. It is my hope that by the time you have turned the final page, you will have gained a sense that I have formed a bond with the people and places that I have photographed and that you are inspired to form your own bonds and bring closer those people, cultures and places that may now seem foreign to you.

—Sidney A. McPhee

本书摄影作品是我近十年来游历中国的劳动结晶，足迹遍及中国六十多个城镇。这些照片反映了美国及世界各地的读者对正在迅速崛起的新兴力量——中国——那份持续升温的兴趣与好奇。这些照片也折射出一位美国大学校长眼里的中国，他一直并将继续致力于与中国各地的机构和个人建立业务和人际往来，积极促进对这个迷人国度的文化理解。

与其他组织领导人一样，大学校长常常要站在"三万英尺"的高度看待问题。从这一高度，可以洞察人与自然进程中共同作用之美，有助于形成对世界的整体印象，也有助于塑造自己的思维与领导方式。作为领导者，从如此高的视角俯看世界，需要面对的挑战是：如何捕捉稍纵即逝的印象，以何种方式传达这些印象，以使处于地面的人参与其中，并为这些印象欢欣鼓舞。本书的目的是要通过照片颂扬中国悠久的历史与往昔的辉煌，激励读者更深入地了解中国、中国的文化与中国的人民，鼓励人们收拾行囊到中国一游，亲身体验这个活力四射的世界大国，亲自体会这个对世界经济、教育与社会文化等方方面面都影响深远的优美国度。

中国是一个魅力四射的国度，这一点毋庸质疑，这主要源于它民族与地形的多样性。尽管我们常说"一个中国"，但"一个"这个词显然不足以描绘这个民风各异、地形多样的多民族国家。正是这种多样性使得中国独具魅力。更为重要的是，这片魅力独具的土地有着悠久的历史与文化。上文提到，本书是我个人旅行的写照，这段旅程开启了我人生新的征程，激励我用全新的视角看待问题、增长见识、加深理解，得到意想不到的收获和难以忘怀的友谊。我希望各位读者朋友看完本书时能意识到我与我拍摄的人物、地点之间已建立起的那种强有力的纽带，希望这种纽带能激发你起程，与这些可爱的人与美丽的地方建立起属于你自己的纽带。我也希望通过这些图片拉近读者朋友与中国的距离，使那些对你来说原本比较陌生的人物、文化与地方不再陌生。

——西德尼·A·麦克菲

作者简介 BIO OF PHOTOGRAPHER

Dr. Sidney A. McPhee is the tenth president of Middle Tennessee State University (MTSU), which is located in Murfreesboro, Tennessee, in the southern United States. A native of Nassau, Bahamas, and an amateur photographer for more than 25 years, he has enjoyed an extensive career in higher education and numerous awards and accolades, including the title of Honorary Professor at China Agricultural University in Beijing (2007). He earned a Bachelor of Arts degree from Prairie View A&M University (Texas); a master's degree from the University of Miami, Coral Gables (Florida); and a doctorate in applied behavioral studies in education from Oklahoma State University (Oklahoma). He is a senior advisor to HANBAN Confucius Institute headquarters. During the past 11 years, Dr. McPhee has visited more than 65 cities within China. He enjoys sharing his photos with others, particularly with the school children that he mentors in Tennessee. He and his wife, Elizabeth, have two adult children, Sidney-Anthony and Seneca.

　　西德尼·A·麦克菲博士是位于美国南部田纳西州默弗里斯伯勒的中田纳西州州立大学（MTSU）的第十任校长，出生于巴哈马拿骚，从事业余摄影已逾25年，长期从事高等教育研究，获奖无数，2007年还被北京中国农业大学授予"名誉教授"头衔。他先后获得德克萨斯州普雷里维农业机械大学文学学士学位，佛罗里达州科勒尔盖布尔斯的迈阿密大学硕士学位以及俄克拉荷马州州立大学教育应用行为研究博士学位，现任国家汉办孔子学院总部的高级顾问。过去的11年间，麦克菲博士访问过中国65座城市。他乐于与人——特别是他指导的田纳西州的学生们——分享自己的摄影作品。麦克菲与妻子伊丽莎白育有两名小孩——西德尼·安东尼和塞内卡，现在都已长大成人。

目录 CONTENTS

A person's face says far more than their mouth...A person's face reflects who he is, what he is feeling, and his aspirations in life.

——German Philosopher

一个人的相貌比他的言辞更能揭示一个人的内心世界。人的相貌不仅仅揭示他的身份与内心感受，更能反映他对生活的热望。

——德国哲学家

PEOPLE
AND
FACES
人物与相貌

Traditionally, China has been perceived in the West through a vast series of stereotypes, including those which suggest that it is unified by a common race and that all Chinese people look alike. With a population of more than 1.3 billion people, which is made up of individuals from many cultures and over 56 minor ethnic groups, China boasts many variations in its people. According to Sinha and Chak (2010), although the majority of the Chinese population is indeed Han Chinese, significant proportions of the population are of different ethnic stock, but most visitors fail to see the great sense of diversity in this huge country because they do not venture beyond the major tourist cities like Beijing and Shanghai.

Demonstrating the diversity of the Chinese people has been a major theme of my photographic efforts over the past decade, and the photographs that I have taken that focus on the faces of Chinese people are among my favorites. American poet Ralph Waldo Emerson is quoted as saying, "Man finds room in the few square inches of the face for the traits of all his ancestors; for the expression of all his history, and his wants." And, I have truly found that the faces of those around us tell the greatest story of their past, present and future. While this book features a variety of different categories of photographs, the faces, actions and expressions of the Chinese people tell the true story of what China is all about and serve as a window into the everyday lives of those who call this magnificent country home.

Photographer's Impressions:

By far, people were my absolute favorite photo subjects in my travels throughout China. It never ceases to amaze me the warmth, kindness and willingness of the majority of Chinese people who gave me permission to take their photograph. Throughout the years, I also observed the practice or custom of Chinese people, from all ages, genders, and regions of the country, flashing the "peace" sign or holding up two fingers like a "V" when a photo is take of them. The photos presented here show the beauty that represents a nation of many faces but one people.

过去，西方社会对中国一直有种刻板印象，认为它是由单一民族构成的。中国人长得都一个样，好像出自同一个模子。事实上，中国人口众多，拥有13多亿人口，由56个民族组成，各民族风俗迥异。辛哈(Sinha)和查克(Chak)（2010）认为，尽管汉族占中国总人口的绝大多数，但是少数民族在中国人口中也占据重要地位。不无遗憾的是，大多数外国游客经常忽视这个泱泱大国的多样性，那是因为他们常驻足于北京，上海这些大城市。

展现中国人民的多样性是我过去十年摄影工作的重要主题，人物摄影更是我的最爱。美国诗人拉尔夫·华尔多·爱默生说："人们在面孔这方寸之地上寻找先辈的痕迹，寻找有关他的历史与希冀的一切信息。"我发现，在我们周围，容貌确确实实向我们诉说着一个人的过去、现在和未来。本书将照片分成中国人的相貌、动作与表情三大类，真实地讲述中国的故事，记录下那些把这块神奇土地称之为"家"的中国人日常生活的点点滴滴。

感言：

到目前为止，人像摄影绝对是我游历中国期间摄影的最爱，因为它不断带给我惊喜。当我提出摄影请求时，大多数中国人都非常热情、友好且非常配合。纵观这些年的摄影作品，我发现，中国人，不论男女老幼，不论是来自乡村还是城市，摄影时都会面带微笑，其唇形类似英文单词"Peace（和平）"的发音，或伸出两根手指比画出"V"的样子。这些图片展现的是一个国家多张面孔之美，他们都来自同一个民族——中华民族。

This photo was taken in 2007 of a working Chinese woman in Zhouzhuang as she operated her water taxi for visitors. I have been impressed with joyfulness and positive attitude expressed through the smiles on the faces of Chinese who are hard at work, as seen in this photo.

经营出租船的中国妇女，2007年摄于周庄。如照片上这位达观的中国妇女一样，中国人民辛勤劳作时脸上绽放的灿烂笑容以及周身洋溢着的愉悦乐观的精神风貌给我留下了深刻印象。

An elderly man photographed in 2010 at the Presidential Palace in Nanjing. He told me through a translator that he was 86 years old, the same age as my mother.

长者，2010年摄于南京总统府。老人通过翻译告诉我，他86岁，与我母亲同岁。

Photographs of reflective Chinese men taken in Hangzhou, Changsha, and Beijing.
沉思静想的中国男子，摄于杭州、长沙、北京三地。

An elderly woman sitting on the side of the street in Suzhou. This was an emotional shot for me because I could sense loneliness and many years of hard work in her face.

苏州街边老妇人。这张照片让我感触颇多，因为从这位老妇人的脸上，我能感受到孤寂落寞与岁月风霜。

Both photos of these elderly Chinese women were taken at Mount Hengshan at Nanyue in Hunan Province and show the beauty and grace of these aged Chinese females.
中国老妇人，摄于湖南衡山。两张照片都显示出中国女性的美丽与优雅。

Another of my favorite photos taken during a visit to Xining Ta'er Monastery. It is one of six famous monasteries in the Yellow Hat Sect of Tibetan Buddhism. Two lamas strolling on the compound, perhaps father and son, one the teacher and the other a willing student in training.

我最喜欢的照片之一，摄于西宁塔尔寺。西宁塔尔寺是中国藏传佛教格鲁派（黄教）六大寺院之一。两名喇嘛，也许是父子，也许是师徒，在院子里漫步。

A handsome reflective young Lama in Xining Taesrsi.

沉思低头的年轻喇嘛，摄于西宁塔尔寺。

Ethnic minority Chinese wearing their cultural costumes for visitors at the Ethnic Group Villages in Shilin, Yuanan Province.
云南石林民俗村，身着少数民族服装的工作人员。

Minority ethnic female tour guides pass the time by using their cell phones as they wait for visitors to come to the village in Shilin, Yuanan Province. The beautiful hats worn by the three ladies have triangle-shaped flaps that differentiate married from single women. If the flaps are up, the person is single, and if it is down, she is married.

云南石林的少数民族女导游。在等待游客的闲暇，女导游们玩手机打发时间。三名妇女头戴着漂亮的花包头，包头上的三角形饰物朝下表明已婚，朝上则表明未婚。

A beautiful Chinese lady dressed in Western style who gladly agreed to pose for this photo taken in Shanghai. I was drawn to her because my wife loves to wear hats.

上海，一位身着洋装靓丽的中国女士欣然接受我的拍摄请求，在镜头前摆出这个造型。我之所以注意到她，是因为我妻子喜欢戴帽子。

A pretty Chinese lady is posing for my camera. Photo was taken in 2010 at the Shanghai World Expo. She reminds me of a cosmopolitan Westerner with her stylish dress.

俏佳人，2010年摄于上海世博会。这位女士让我想到着装时尚的大都会西方妇女。

Photos of these new married couples were taken on the streets of Shanghai. The younger Chinese generation arrange for both a Western style and a traditional Chinese wedding. These photos show the Western style wedding.

新婚夫妇，摄于上海街头。中国现如今的年轻人会筹办兼具中西特色的婚礼。这些照片显示的是西式婚礼。

During my visit to Dunhuang, the Mayor of the city along with a host of city officials, local television reporters, cameramen, photographers, and others accompanied me on a leisurely stroll through the night market. Off course, my entourage and I created a buzz among the merchants and locals who were enjoying the evening.

The next morning, I decided to revisit the area again without the mass entourage. I was accompanied this time with only the former President of Northwest Normal University, President Wang, who was a good friend of the Mayor of Dunhuang. As we took an early morning walk down the street that we had visited the night before, I stopped to get my shoes shined. As I was being taken care of, I noticed that President Wang was engaged in a very heated conversation, in Chinese, with a female merchant.

On our way back to the hotel, I asked President Wang what was the heated conversation about. He told me that the female merchant was telling him that I was "a big boss from South Africa, with nine wives who was looking at making a major investment in Dunhuang." President Wang tried to tell her that I was a good friend who was a university President from America. She did not believe him and insisted that she and the other merchants were right about who I was and the word had spread throughout the city.

Needless to say, when I recounted this story to my wife upon returning to America, she was not amused. She banned me from ever visiting Dunhuang again. Actually, I can visit the city again, only with my only wife.

　　访问敦煌期间，我在敦煌市市长、市政官员、当地电视台记者、摄像师、摄影师以及其他工作人员的陪同下，漫步在敦煌夜市街头。我与随行人员会时不时地停下来与商人及当地人攀谈，度过了一个愉快的夜晚。

　　第二天一早，我决定在没有大批随行人员的陪同下再次光顾这一地区。这一次，陪同我前往的只有好朋友，西北师范大学前任校长王利民博士，他也是敦煌市市长的好朋友。清晨，我们再次漫步夜市街头，我停下来请人刷了刷皮鞋。在我刷鞋时，我注意到王校长用中文与一名女商人聊得火热。

　　在回酒店的路上，我好奇地问王校长与女商人聊什么聊得那么火热。他告诉我：女商人说我是来自南非的大老板，有九个妻子，正准备在敦煌做一项重大投资。王校长试图告诉她，我是他的好朋友，是一位美国大学校长，她却不相信，并坚称，她和其他商人对我的背景了如指掌，有关我的故事已传遍大街小巷，尽人皆知。

　　不用说，返回美国后，当我跟妻子讲起这个故事时，她很不开心。她不准我再次访问敦煌。我当然可以再次访问敦煌，前提条件是只能妻子一人作陪。

In every city of China one can see hard working Chinese who do what is necessary to get the job done and to get the goods delivered.
在中国每一座城市都可以看到辛勤工作的中国人，他们尽心尽力完成每一项工作，将货物运抵每一个目的地。

A Chinese father with his daughter as they enjoy viewing the photographer's exhibition in 2010 held at China Agricultural University campus in Beijing.
欣赏摄影作品的华裔父女。2010年，本人摄影作品展在北京中国农业大学校园内举行。

Mother and daughter relaxing after a long day at the 2010 Shanghai World Expo.
小憩。母女俩在2010年上海世博会尽情游玩一日后稍事休息。

A young Hangzhou Normal University student who was a translator and guide during my visits to the 2010 Shanghai World Expo, the Confucius Temple in Nanjing, and the French concession area of Shanghai.

年轻的杭州师范大学学生。这名学生在我参观2010年上海世博会、南京夫子庙和上海法租界期间担任我的翻译兼向导。

International friendship. A Chinese lady in Lanzhou was practicing her Tai Chi in the local park and took the time to teach, a foreigner, a friend of the photographer, "how to do it right." Good physical fitness is very important to the Chinese people and the Chinese government. Each morning you will find large groups, particularly seniors, exercising in the local public parks and utilizing exercise equipment there provided by their local and provincial officials.

国际友谊。一位中国老太太正在兰州一家公园内练太极拳，并耐心教授一名外国人——我的一位朋友——"如何做才是正确的。"中国民众和中国政府非常重视健身。每天早晨都能看见许多人，特别是老年人，你一堆，我一群的在公园锻炼，利用公园内由地方和省政府部门提供的运动器材健身。

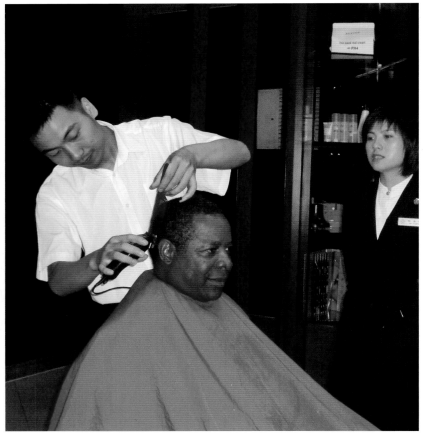

The Photographer receiving his first haircut in China. The Chinese barber was at a hair salon at the hotel in Changsha. It took three Chinese translators, the General manager of the hotel, the assistant general manager, and my Chinese university host, to communicate to the barber how to cut my hair. To say the least, I was very nervous and worried about the outcome and final product...so was the barber. In the end, I was a very satisfied customer and the barber was so proud of his work that he requested to take a picture with me when he was finished. I gladly agreed and now my picture hangs in his salon. He told me through the translator that I was the first black person whose hair he cut and that he was honored to do so.

我在中国第一次理发。这名中国理发师供职于长沙某酒店美发沙龙。为了告诉理发师我希望剪什么样的发型，共动用了三名中国翻译、一位酒店总经理、一位酒店总经理助理和诚邀我来华的中国大学的一名工作人员。可以毫不夸张地说，我当时的确有些惴惴不安，担心发型不能尽如人意。理发师也很紧张。最后，我非常满意自己的发型，理发师也为自己的最终作品而洋洋自得并要求与我合影留念，我欣然同意。现在我与他的合照就挂在这家美发沙龙里。他通过翻译告诉我，我是他第一位黑人顾客，他感到很荣幸。

A photo-op with the local farmer who claims to have discovered the Terra Cotta ruins while digging for water well in the Xi'an area.

与当年在西安地区挖水井时发现了兵马俑遗址的农民朋友合影留念。

A calligrapher at the night market in Dunhuang presenting me with my Chinese name, Zhao Meilong as my adopted Chinese name, given to me by a good Chinese friend from Changsha.

敦煌夜市一位书法家赠予写有我中国名字"赵美龙"的书法作品。"赵美龙"是我长沙一位要好的中国朋友给我取的中文名字。

CHILDREN
中国孩童

It's all but impossible to look into the face of a happy, healthy child without smiling. And, Chinese children, like those from most other cultures, evoke smile after smile because of their great curiosity of the world around them and their amazing ability to find joy in the simplest of things and total fulfillment in the people that they love. Like their older counterparts, Chinese children are also a diverse lot, who enjoy playing, exploring their surroundings and learning about their own culture as well as that of others. The time that Chinese parents spend in caring for and teaching their children is very evident, and a considerable amount of emphasis is placed on teaching them to not only learn and appreciate the value and traditions of the Chinese culture but also to understand the language and customs of others. My ability to photograph the beautiful children that are featured in this section of the book is quite reflective of the friendliness of their parents and their willingness to having their children interact with individuals of other backgrounds and cultures.

Photographer's Impressions:

Without a doubt, having the opportunity to interact with young Chinese children was always a special experience in my many visits to China, in both urban and rural areas. I recall, with great fondness, one such encounter in 2006 during a visit to Wu wei, where I met a small group of Chinese children playing near a cultural site. On that occasion, a young boy came up to me and gave me a crumpled piece of paper, and on it, written in English, was "Welcome to China — I love you."

看着孩子们那一张张洋溢着幸福与健康的脸庞，谁都会发出会心的微笑。中国孩子，与其他许多国家的孩子一样，总是笑声不断，对身边的世界充满好奇，能从最简单的事物中找寻到快乐，更得益于他们所爱的人让他们获得的那份巨大满足感。像父辈们一样，中国的孩子们也是各具特点，尽情嬉戏，努力探索周遭的一切，积极学习本民族及异域文化知识。

中国家长在照顾和教育小孩方面所花费的时间与精力之多，是有目共睹的。教育时，他们不仅重视孩子们对中国本土文化的传承与发扬，也强调对外语与异域风俗习惯的理解。本节的主角是这些天真可爱的中国孩子，这应归功于孩子家长的友善与合作，因为他们愿意让自己的孩子与文化背景迥异的人交往，才使得拍摄成为可能。

感言：

毫无疑问，能够有机会与中国孩子交往，是我多次访问中国的特殊经历，无论这些孩子是来自僻远的农村还是繁华的都市。记得2006年访问武威时正巧遇到一群孩子在一个文化遗址附近玩耍。一个小男孩走过来，递给我一张皱巴巴的纸，上面用英文写着："欢迎您来到中国——我爱你！"

A young, beautiful Chinese girl photographed in Nanjing, China in 2010. Check out the pearl necklace she is wearing.
年少漂亮的中国女孩，2010年摄于中国南京。值得注意的是小女孩还戴着一串珍珠项链。

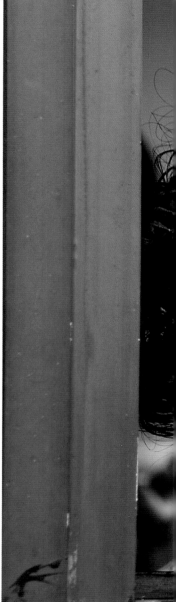

Two cute little girls dressed in traditional Chinese pajamas. Photo was taken in Suzhou.
身着中国传统服饰的两名可爱的小女孩，摄于苏州。

This photo is one of my all-time favorites. It was taken in 2006 outside of Zhouzhuang at a restaurant. The beauty of this child was striking and reflective of the innocence and wonder of so many of the Chinese children that I have had the opportunity to photograph. Again, this hairstyle reminds me of my daughter when she was this age.

这张照片是我的最爱之一，2006年摄于周庄餐厅外。这个可爱的孩子让人过目不忘，有着众多中国孩子的那份纯真与好奇。与此同时，这个发型让我想起我女儿在她这个年龄时的样子。

I have always asked for permission from parents to take pictures of their children. This photo was taken around Heng Mountain in Hunan Province. I put my Middle Tennessee State University hat on the child. He is now ready for college in America.

我总是征求孩子父母的同意让我可以拍摄他们孩子的照片。这张照片摄于湖南衡山。我把中田纳西州州立大学的帽子戴在孩子头上。他现在准备到美国读大学。

A brother and sister in Shanghai near the French concession area.
姐弟俩，摄于上海法租界区附近。

A boy in Chengde—a very scenic area of China. He was playing with his friends near the lake.
与朋友在湖边嬉戏的男孩。摄于承德——中国一个风景如画的地方。

A boy in Suzhou who knows how to pose for a photo.
苏州男孩，他知道如何摆出漂亮的造型。

A little girl from Kunming with a personality for the camera.
镜头前个性十足的昆明小女孩。

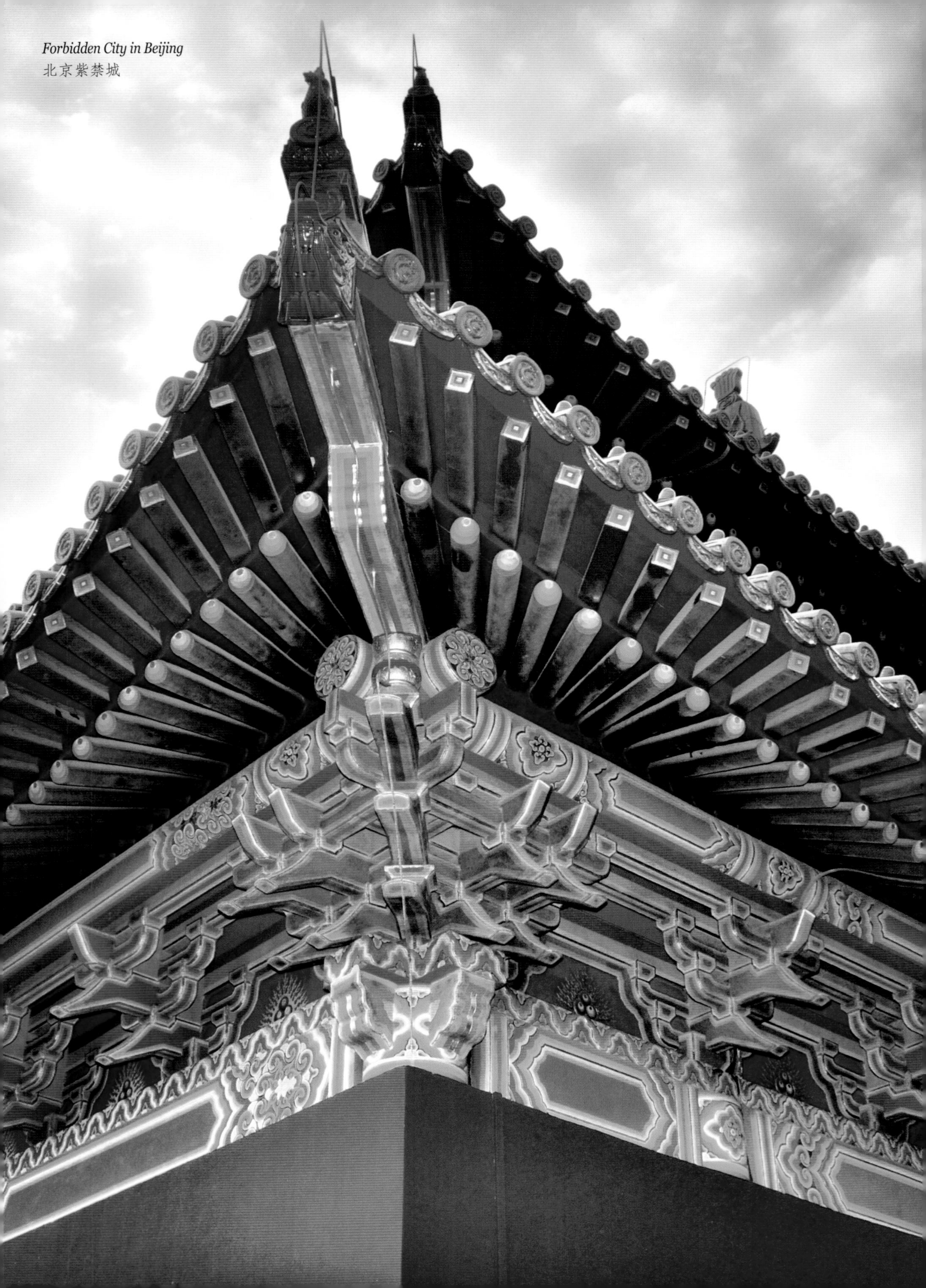
Forbidden City in Beijing
北京紫禁城

HISTORICAL
&
CULTURAL SITES
历史名胜

In spite of the changing perception of China as a more modern and innovative country, few people would deny the significance of the longstanding history and cultural traditions that have served as a primary trademark for this remarkable nation. Recorded Chinese culture dates back more than 3,000 years ago to the Zhou Dynasty and its cultural heritage is considered one of the oldest and most complex in the world. Out of this storied history remain countless historic relics and time-honored customs and traditions, which have become popular targets for professional and amateur photographers alike.

Photographer's Impressions:

China's historical sites rival those of any developed nation in the world. The beauty, serenity and majesty of China's numerous historic landmarks make them a must-see for visitors and the local Chinese people alike. The value, respect and care that the Chinese government (both provincial and the Central) has given to the historic preservation of various cultural relics and sites is quite evident, and considerable resources have been allocated to the maintenance and upkeep of the various sites. China has every right to be proud of those places and landmarks that not only hold cultural significance for its people but also serve to attract thousands upon thousands of tourists and other guests to China each year.

随着中国近年来的迅猛发展，今日之中国已崛起成为一个更具现代化、更具创新活力的国家，但是，几乎没有人会对这个国家悠久的历史与文化传统视而不见。正是因为其悠久的历史与文化才使得中国屹于世界文化之林。中国有文献记载的文化可上溯到三千多年前的周朝，直至今天仍被认为是世界上最古老和最复杂的文化遗产之一。除文献资料外，中国还有数不胜数的历史遗迹和古老的风俗习惯，所有这些都深深吸引着专业和业余摄影爱好者的眼球，急切地想把它们摄入镜头。

感言：

中国历史遗迹可与任何发达国家的历史遗迹相媲美。中国众多的历史名胜以其优美、恬静、宏伟吸引着世界各地的游人，成为国内外观光者和当地人必看的景点。中国中央政府及地方政府十分重视历史文化遗址的保护，投入大量的资金和人力维护和修缮众多文化遗址。中国完全有权力为拥有这些历史景点及标志性建筑而自豪，这些历史景点与标志性建筑是民族的，也是世界的，它们不仅对本民族人民具有重要的非比寻常的文化价值，每年还吸引着数以万计的中外游客参观访问中国。

The Forbidden City is a massive architectural wonder. It shows the genius of the ancient Chin... ... the Imperial Palace and living quarters for twenty...

北京紫禁城，一个宏大的建筑奇观，它显示了古代中国人民的聪明才智。这座皇宫是明、清两代二十四位帝王的皇宫，...

The radiance of the Temple of Heaven, one of the most visited historical sites in Beijing.
北京天坛，著名历史遗迹之一。

The ceiling and interior of a pavilion in the Summer Palace complex in Beijing.
北京颐和园展馆内部及其天花板。

Tian'anmen Square and the Forbidden City in Beijing. This photo was taken during National Day in 2010. The area was beautifully decorated with real colorful flowers. It is one of the largest public squares in the world.
北京天安门广场和紫禁城。照片摄于2010年国庆。整个广场被五颜六色的鲜花装点得格外美丽。天安门广场是世界上最大的城市中心广场之一。

This photo depicts the splendor of the Forbidden City in Beijing.
金碧辉煌的北京紫禁城。

This photo of the Great Wall in Beijing. Over the years, I have visited the Great Wall many times and have taken numerous pictures there. This photo is special because I waited over two hours to get this shot without any tourists or workers in the photo. It was a beautiful morning in May, 2008.

北京长城。多年来，我数度游览长城，拍摄了多张长城照片。这张照片拍摄于2008年五月一个美丽的早晨，其独特之处在于，我苦等了两个多小时，终于等到没有任何游人或工人的身影出现在照片中。

These photos of the Terra Cotta Warriors in Xi'an are breathtaking. The museum and active archeological sites must be part of a traveler's itinerary when visiting China.

On one of my several visits to Xi'an and the Terra Cotta Museum, I had the honor and pleasure of meeting the local Chinese farmer who discovered the artifacts upon digging a well in search of water.

令人叹为观止的西安秦始皇兵马俑。参观博物馆和考古遗址是我游览中国必不可少的行程之一。

我多次参观西安兵马俑博物馆，有一次我有幸见到一位当年为寻找水源去打水井而意外发现兵马俑的当地

Terra Cotta Museum, Xi'an.
西安兵马俑博物馆。

Terra Cotta Warriors Museum, Xi'an
西安兵马俑博物馆。

A chariot with soldier at the Terra Cotta Museum in Xi'an.
战车与兵士俑，摄于西安兵马俑博物馆。

The Tian Ti Shan Buddha and Grottoes in Wuwei, North China. This is one of the largest Buddha statues in China.
天梯山石佛与石窟。摄于甘肃武威。这尊佛像是中国最大的佛像之一。

A golden Buddha near the Great Wild Goose Pagoda in Xi'an.
西安大雁塔附近的金佛。

The pagoda at North Temple in Suzhou. Pagodas can be found throughout China, reflecting the vast influence of Buddhism imported from India and other Eastern countries. I have often heard the saying that "India developed Buddhism and China practices it".

苏州北寺塔。佛塔遍及中国大江南北，反映出佛教对中国民众的巨大影响。佛教从印度及其他东方国家传入中国。我经常听人说："佛教起源于印度，却在中国发扬光大。"

The Great Wild Goose Pagoda in Xi'an. It is an imposing structure with great character.

气势恢弘的西安大雁塔。

A statue of the great Chinese Philosopher, Confucius. This photo was taken at the Confucian Temple in Nanjing, China. I visited the Temple in October 2010 on the evening of Confucius' birthday.

南京夫子庙之孔子雕像。孔子是中国伟大的哲学家。我于2010年10月孔子诞辰日当晚参观了夫子庙。

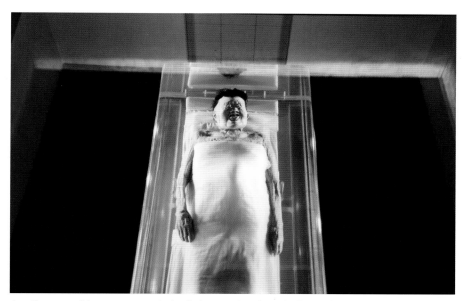

A well preserved human corpse of Xin Zhui, Marquise of Dai (nicknamed Lady Dai), displayed at the Hunan Provincial Museum in the city of Changsha. She died in 186 B.C. which makes her over 2000 years old. The corpse was excavated in Han Tombs at Mawangdui. I took this photo during my visit to China in 2008 when I attended the Beijing Olympics.

保存完好的辛追夫人古尸，出土于马王堆汉墓，现陈列于长沙湖南省博物馆。辛追夫人又称"轪侯夫人"或"侯爵夫人"，死于公元前186年，距今2000多年。照片拍摄于2008年我前往中国参加北京奥运会途中。

Acrobatic performance in Beijing. I have seen the most incredible athletic and acrobatic performances in China than in any other parts of the world that I have traveled.

北京杂技表演。在中国，我看过比世界其他地区更精妙绝伦的体育和杂技表演。

CULTURAL AND ACROBATIC PERFORMANCES
文化与体育盛事

Experiencing the arts and culture of China is a treat for each of the senses. In almost every location, you find unique musical performances, colorful costumes and dramatic scenery, the taste and smell of unimaginable culinary delicacies, and the unforgettable textures of everything from exotic cloth to one's natural surroundings. Truly, a person cannot understand China without experiencing what is culturally unique to this nation, including outstanding performances by beautiful dancers in brilliant costumes, the unique sounds of authentic Chinese instruments and song, and extravagant productions performed flawlessly by Chinese men and women who demonstrate that their performance is more than just their craft, but it is also a traditional part of life.

Photographer's Impressions:

Over the years, I have been fortunate to attend many cultural events and performances all around the world. During my many extensive trips to China, I have seen nearly 15 different cultural and acrobatic performances, including: The Impression West Lake and Guilin The Show of Impression Liu Sanjie, directed by the world famous producer, director and cinematographer Zhang Yimou (who also directed the opening and closing ceremonies of the 2008 Olympics in Beijing); the Tang Dynasty in Xi'an; the Beautiful Girls of Dunhuang; the Peking Opera; and the Charming Hunan performance in Zhangjiajie, just to name a few. From my perspective, the Chinese cultural shows are unmatched by any standards. The singers, performers, staging, lighting, and every aspect of the show, are absolutely outstanding, and the athletic and acrobatic talents displayed in many of the performances are unlike anything you would see anywhere in the world. I have yet to be disappointed after attending a Chinese cultural show.

细心品味中国的艺术与文化真是感官的一大享受。在中国各地，你都能发现魅力独特的音乐表演、色彩纷呈的戏剧服装和美轮美奂的舞台布景，闻到各种美食的诱人香味，品尝到各式各样难以想象的美食，看到令人难以忘怀的纹理——小到具有异国风情的布料、大到自然的山川都能看到这种奇丽的纹理。一个人如果想要真正了解中国，就必须亲身体验这个神奇国度特有的文化，亲眼观赏衣着奢华艳丽的美丽舞者表演的戏剧，亲耳聆听正宗中国乐器与歌曲的独特韵律，亲手把玩完美无瑕的艺术品——这些手工艺品展示出中国手工艺人们精湛的技艺，也是传统生活的一部分。

感言：

这些年来，我有幸参加世界各地的许多文化盛事和演出。在中国旅游期间，我欣赏过15场文化和杂技演出，例如：由世界著名制作人、导演和电影摄影师张艺谋执导的"西湖印象"和桂林的"印象刘三姐"（张艺谋还是2008北京奥运会开幕式及闭幕式的总导演），西安的"大唐王朝"，"敦煌飞天美女"，京剧以及张家界的"魅力湖南"等。在我看来，中国的文化演出是无法用特定标准去衡量的。歌手、演员、舞台、灯光以及演出的方方面面都美轮美奂，无与伦比。许多文艺演出中体育人才与杂技高手云集，其高超的技艺让人耳目一新。迄今为止，还从没有哪一场中国文化演出让我失望过。

I have attended numerous cultural performances in China. This photo shows the face changing which is a tour de force of Sichuan drama art. The picture was taken at a cultural performance in Beijing.

我观看过多场中国的文艺演出。这张照片摄于北京文化汇演，展示的是四川戏剧艺术的一大杰作——"变脸"。

The Tang Dynasty Cultural performance in Xi'an. The costumes, props, music and acting are exceptional.
西安唐朝文化演出。从服饰、道具、音乐到表演都精妙绝伦。

A grand cultural performance of the Charming Xiangxi Hunan show at Zhangjiajie area in Hunan Province. This was one of the more colorful and dramatic shows I have ever experienced.

湖南张家界地区盛大的"魅力湘西"文艺演出，这是我见过的最丰富多彩、最激动人心的文艺演出之一。

Excited children on a field trip to the 2010 Shanghai World Expo. They absolutely enjoyed posing for my camera.

赶赴2010年上海世博会的兴奋的孩子们。他们喜欢在我的相机前摆出各种造型。

EDUCATION
&
PARTNERSHIPS
教育合作伙伴关系

Without question, education is an important part of Chinese culture. As a country, China has invested heavily in the education of its people, which is reflected in the fact that more than 90 percent of its population is literate, from individuals in its most remote peasant villages to its most modern, bustling cities (Powell, 2009). The country has also invested in building educational relationships with other countries around the world in an effort to enhance worldwide understanding and appreciation for the Chinese culture and its people.

As a university president, some of my most rewarding experiences have involved my engagement and interaction with Chinese universities and the academic partnerships that have developed. These exchanges have not only provided significant opportunities for me to learn more about the value of education for the Chinese people but to also use photography to share in the experience of educating others about the great land of China. If "a nation's treasure is in its scholars" as the Chinese proverb suggests, China is, indeed, rich beyond measure and those who have been fortunate enough to engage in collaborative educational programs and projects with the Chinese have themselves become richer for the experience.

Photographer's Impressions:

It is very clear to any outsider that the Chinese government and its people place a very high value on education at all levels. I have been impressed with the financial resources allocated by the local Provincial and Central Government to support Chinese colleges and universities. As an educator, I have also observed, with a great sense of appreciation and fondness, the commitment, devotion, and competitiveness demonstrated by Chinese college students towards their education. I have lectured throughout China, and I am always amazed by the large attendance and enthusiasm of Chinese students to my lectures and speeches. In every setting, students exhibited a hunger for knowledge and a great appreciation for the opportunity to learn more about individuals of other cultures and nations.

教育无疑是中国文化的重要组成部分。中国投入巨资提高国民素质，不论是最现代、最繁华的大都市还是最偏远的农村，超过90%的人都接受过识字教育（鲍威尔，2009）。中国投入资金，积极建立与世界各国的教育合作关系以促进世界对中国文化及中国人民的了解与欣赏。

作为一名大学校长，与中国大学及其学术合作伙伴的交流与互动让我受益匪浅。这些交流活动不仅使我得以更深入地了解中国人民的教育理念，也令我有机会运用现代摄影技术与他人分享中国这块伟大土地的教育经验。中国有句谚语："学者众则国富。"以此观之，中国财富之多难以估量。如果有幸与他们在教育规划与项目方面展开合作必将收益良多。

感言：

中国政府和中国民众非常重视各级教育，这一点世人皆知。我印象最深的是各地政府及中央政府投入大量资金支持中国高校发展。作为一名教育工作者，我特别欣羡中国大学生手不释卷，不甘人后的学习态度。我在中国各地演讲，每每惊诧于中国大学生听讲座或演讲的人数之多以及热情之高。在中国，随时随地你都能看到学生们如饥似渴地汲取知识，不愿错过每一个了解异域文化的机会。

Signing ceremony at China Agricultural University (CAU) of partnership with Middle Tennessee State University in Murfreesboro, Tennessee, U.S.A. This agreement was one of the first to be signed with a Chinese university. The President of CAU at that time was Dr. Chen Zhangliang. He is now Vice Governor of Guangxi Province and one of my best friends.

中国农业大学（CAU）与美国田纳西州默弗里斯伯勒的中田纳西州州立大学就建立教育合作伙伴关系举行的签约仪式。这份协议是中田纳西州州立大学与中国内地大学最早签署的协议之一。当时中国农业大学校长是陈章良博士，现为广西省副省长，是我最要好的朋友之一。

The Entrance Gate of Hunan Normal University in Changsha. Middle Tennessee State University has partnered with this university in many areas such as study abroad/exchange programs and faculty and administrator exchange initiatives.

长沙湖南师范大学校门。中田纳西州州立大学与湖南师范大学在出国留学生、交换生以及教师与行政人员交流等诸多领域展开合作。

Meeting with the Director of International Affairs office at Northwest Normal University (NWNU) to discuss strengthening the partnership between NWNU and Middle Tennessee State University. Director Quan has been a great advocate for improving educational partnerships between NWNU and MTSU.

与西北师范大学（NWNU）国际合作交流处处长会面，共同商讨如何增强西北师范大学与中田纳西州州立大学的教育合作伙伴关系。西北师大国际合作交流处权处长积极推进两校间的教育合作伙伴关系。

The photographer receiving in 2010 the Honorary Title of Consultant and Senior Adviser to Hanban and Confucius Institute Headquarters in Beijing.

2010年，本人接受北京国家汉办和孔子学院总部授予的高级顾问荣誉称号。

Speech on globalization at Hangzhou Normal University in Hangzhou, China. I have delivered many speeches and lectures in China.
在杭州师范大学做有关全球化的演讲。在中国，我做过多场演讲与讲座。

The audience listens intently as the photographer delivers a lecture at China Agricultural University in Beijing just prior to being awarded in 2007 the "Distinguished Professor" title, one of the highest academic honors, by the university.
听众们认真倾听本人在北京中国农业大学所做的讲座。在此之前，本人于2007年刚刚被中国农业大学授予"名誉教授"称号，这是该校颁发的最高学术荣誉之一。

Opening ceremony of photographer's photo exhibition and lecture on the campus of Hangzhou Normal University in 2010.
在杭州师范大学校园举办的本人摄影作品展的开幕式上，摄于2010年。

Opening ceremony of photographer's photo exhibition on the campus of Hunan Normal University in Changsha in 2010.
在长沙湖南师范大学校园举办的本人摄影作品展的开幕式上，摄于2010年。

欢迎美国中田纳西州立大学Sidney McPhee校长
Welcome President Sidney McPhee,
Middle Tennessee State University, U.S.A.

2010年05月
星期三
上午 11:

Dr. Xu Liu, Chief Executive Officer of Hanban/Confucius Institute Headquarters in Beijing.
许琳博士，北京国家汉办及孔子学院总部总干事。

The photographer being presented with a gift, a photo book on China, by Dr. Xu Lin, Chief Executive officer of Hanban/ Confucius Institute Headquarters in Beijing. It was during this presentation, at the Hanban headquarters, shortly after a lecture and PowerPoint showing of the photograph's work, Dr. Xu Lin suggested that the photographer publish his photos taken over the past ten years. The idea for this photo book was born from her suggestion and support.

北京国家汉办主任、孔子学院总部总干事许琳博士赠予本人一本有关中国的摄影集。这组照片摄于国家汉办总部，本人刚刚结束讲座，讲座时用PPT展示了自己的摄影作品。许博士建议本人将过去十年拍摄的照片结集出版。这本摄影集的问世得益于她的建议和大力支持。

A statue of the great Chinese Philosopher, Confucius. This photo was taken at the entrance of the Yuelu Academy, one of China's oldest institutions of higher learning in Changsha, Hunan Province.
岳麓书院入口处的孔子雕像。岳麓书院位于湖南省长沙市，是中国最古老的书院之一。

The gate at the entrance of China Agricultural University campus in Beijing.
北京中国农业大学入口处的大门。

Lecture at Guangxi Normal University in Nanning, China
在中国南宁广西师范大学讲座时的情景

Signing partnership agreements with the Presidents of Hangzhou Normal University and Hunan Normal University.
与杭州师范大学及湖南师范大学校长签署合作协议。

Lecture on internationalization by the photographer at Hangzhou Normal University.
在杭州师范大学做有关国际化的讲座。

Meeting in Hangzhou with exchange students from Hangzhou Normal University prior to their enrollment at Middle Tennessee State University in Murfreesboro, Tennessee, U.S.A.
在杭州与即将赴美国田纳西州默弗里斯伯勒的中田纳西州州立大学作交换生的杭州师范大学的学生见面。

Group of third grade elementary school children at the Discovery School in Murfreesboro, Tennessee, USA. These children are posing with Ms. Elizabeth McPhee, their third grade teacher, their Principal, and their Chinese language instructor who teaches them Chinese. This Chinese language program is sponsored by the Confucius Institute and HANBAN.
与一群美国田纳西州默弗里斯伯勒小学三年级的孩子们摄于科学课上。与孩子们一起合影的有伊丽莎白·麦克菲女士、三年级老师、该校校长以及他们的中文教师。该校汉语语言项目由国家汉办和孔子学院联合赞助。

Detian Waterfall in Guangxi Province. It is the largest waterfall in Asia and is located on the border of Vietnam.

广西德天瀑布，位于中越边境，是亚洲最大的瀑布。

NATURE AND LANDSCAPES
自然风光

"Some people ask me why I want to live in this mountain forest. I just smile and do not answer. My heart feels very peaceful and happy. The flowing water carries floating peach blossoms far away. This is a special, beautiful place. Living here I feel that I am not in the world of mortals." —— Chinese poet Li Bai

During my many visit to China, few things have impacted me as much as the sheer beauty of the Chinese landscape and the connection that the Chinese people seem to have with nature. A Chinese proverb declares that "a bit of fragrance clings to the hand that gives flowers", and I can truly say that China gives something fragrant and beautiful to each person who has the opportunity to experience and explore the vibrantly diverse Chinese landscape. As I have photographed the natural beauty of this very broad country, I have discovered that it is impossible to choose one word that exactly represents all of what an individual might encounter in exploring the land of China. Just as the people of China are diverse and multifaceted, so is the land that they inhabit. You can find everything from lush, green farmlands to dry, sandy deserts or towering majestic mountains to beautiful, scenic plains. From beaches to busy byways, China has it all. And while this collection of very unique environmental settings make for a very different and contrasting backdrop virtually everywhere you go in the country, you somehow always maintain the feeling that every scenic element is connected and that it is a part of the overall natural harmony that is considered so much a part of China.

Photographer's Impressions:

Included within this set of photographs of the incredible natural landscape of China is a photo that was taken during my initial visit to China before the days of the now popular digital camera. My Chinese friend, Dr. Renjie Dong, Director of Internal Programs and Professor at China Agricultural University, accompanied me while cruising the Yangtze. Dr. Dong is the person who introduced me to China in August of 2000. While the "cruise boat" was not the most modern, it was one of the most peaceful and "out of this world" experiences of my life. I cruised the Yangtze the year prior to the construction project of raising the water level to prevent flooding of the area. Since it was my first visit outside of the "big cities of China", I was introduced to "rural China". I had not adjusted to Chinese food so my diet during the three-day cruise of the Yangtze was Chinese beer and Oreo cookies for breakfast, lunch, and dinner. During the cruise, I had the opportunity to visit some of the local villages and interact with the local people. I was pleasantly surprised to find out how friendly, curious, and accepting the people were to foreigners like me. I observed how particularly intrigued they were to meet me and take pictures with me. I later learned that many local Chinese from the rural areas had not met a black person, particularly from America. (Most of them thought that I was from Africa.) The landscape of the Li River in Guilin, which is featured in this section, is very representative of the overall beauty, diversity, peacefulness, cleanliness, and vastness of the incredible natural landscape of China.

"问余何事栖碧山，笑而不答心自闲。 桃花流水杳然去，别有天地非人间。" —— 中国诗人李白

我多次访问中国，中国风光那种超凡绝伦的美以及中国人与自然的和谐令我印象深刻。中国有句谚语："赠人玫瑰，手有余香。"我可以毫不夸张地说，中国将芬芳与美丽带给了每一位有机会亲身体验生动多彩的中国大自然风光的人。在拍摄这个幅员辽阔的国度的自然美景时，我发现无法找到一个合适的词来准确形容在中国的所见所闻。中华民族习俗各异，风情万种，中华大地也是姿态万千、色彩斑斓、令你目不暇接。在中国，从郁郁葱葱的农田，到干旱、黄沙满天的沙漠，从巍峨雄伟的山脉到优美秀丽的平原，从一望无边的海滩到熙熙攘攘的大街小巷，你都能捕捉到美的踪影。这些形态各异，明暗不同的风景构成了一幅幅独特的自然背景。中国人强调和谐之美，迈步在中国的每一寸土地，你总能感受到每一个风光元素与大自然的完美结合。

感言：

在这一组美得让人难以置信的中国自然风光照片中，有一张是我首次访问中国时拍摄的，当时数码摄影还未盛行。我的中国朋友，中国农业大学国际交流与合作处处长董仁杰博士陪着我游览长江。董博士于2000年8月将我引荐到中国。虽然当时我们乘坐的"游船"还不够先进，这次旅行却是我感觉最安逸的旅行之一，让我有种"飘然世外"之感。这次巡游长江是在三峡大坝开工建设的前一年，长江水位还未提高，许多景点还未被江水淹没。这是我第一次目睹"都市中国"以外的天地，真实地接触到"乡村中国"。当时，我还未适应中国的饮食习惯，所以在为期三天的航行中，我一日三餐吃的都是奥利奥饼干和中国啤酒。这次旅游期间，我得以参观当地的一些村庄并与当地人民互动。令我感到惊喜的是，当地人对像我这样的外来客既友善又好奇。他们争相与我合影留念，后来才知道，中国农村地区的很多当地人从未见过黑人，特别是来自美国的黑人，他们中很多人认为我来自非洲。本章的特色是桂林漓江风光，这儿风景秀丽、形态万千、安逸舒缓、干净整洁却又不失宏伟壮丽，是中国自然风光的典范。

The Yellow Mountain in Anhui Province is one of the most beautiful and famous in all of China and the perhaps the world from the photographer's perspective.

安徽黄山，中国最美丽、最著名的山脉之一。在本人看来，黄山或许也是全球最美丽的大山之一。

The Yellow Mountain in Anhui Province—one of nature's scenic wonders in China.
安徽黄山，中国最美的自然奇观之一。

Early morning at the Yellow Mountain in Anhui Province.
安徽黄山清晨。

A photo of the Yangtze River. This photo was taken the year before the water level was raised to address flooding.
长江。照片摄于三峡大坝开工建设的前一年，当时，长江水位还未抬升。

Scenes of the Li River in Guangxi Autonomous region. In America, we refer to scenes like those that one would see during a boat cruise down the Li River as being in "God's Country".

广西壮族自治区漓江风光。乘舟沿漓江而下，两岸风光旖旎，山峰林立、碧水萦回，人行江上宛若置身"神的国度"。

The beautiful Zhangjiajie area in Hunan Province.
湖南省美丽的张家界自然风光。

The mountains of Zhangjiajie where scenes from the successful blockbuster movie Avatar was shot.

张家界群山，电影商业大片《阿凡达》在此取景。

The snow capped mountains on the road to Huanglong. I travelled up this mountain in a sports utility vehicle with the former President Wang Limin of Northwest Normal University (NWNU) and the Director Quan of International Affairs Office of NWNU. I reached the peak of the mountain at 5,000 meters above sea level and did not get sick. I then convinced myself that I was ready for the mountains of Tibet.

雪山，摄于前往黄龙的路上。我与西北师范大学前校长王利民、西北师范大学国际合作与交流处权处长，乘坐一辆运动型多功能车登上此山。登上海拔5000米的山峰，我未感到任何不适，这使我相信我完全有能力征服西藏群山。

Various photos of scenes around Dunhuang. This desert-like area of China shows the diversity of landscape in this vast nation.
敦煌风光。这片类似沙漠的地区显示出广袤的中国大地自然景观的多样性。

The historical City of Dunghuang is well known and a Chinese treasure. It is a beautiful desert oasis.
历史文化名城敦煌，美丽的沙漠绿洲。敦煌名扬天下，是中华民族的瑰宝。

The Mayor of Dunhuang was my host and showed me the gracious hospitality of the City and its people.
东道主敦煌市市长让我充分感受到中国人民和中国城市的热情好客。

I enjoy photographing bridges near lakes and rivers. This is a bridge in Zhouzhuang, also known as the Venice of Asia. Watertown in Zhouzhuang.

水城周庄。我喜欢拍摄湖边或河边的桥。这是周庄的一座小桥，周庄又被称作"亚洲的威尼斯"。

A sunset photo of the West Lake in Hangzhou, China. Hangzhou and the West Lake are known as "Heaven on Earth". I like to refer to Hangzhou as "The Beverly Hills of China".

落日余晖下的西湖，中国杭州。杭州与西湖被称为"人间天堂"，我喜欢称杭州为"中国的比佛利山庄"。

Modern shopping mall in Changsha, Hunan Province
湖南长沙现代气派的商场。

ARCHITECTURE, SKYLINES AND CHINA AT NIGHT
建筑，天际线与夜幕下的中国

One cannot truly appreciate contemporary China without recognizing the beauty and magnificence of its modern skyline and its architecture. In recent years, TravelersDigest.com ranked the "futuristic" skyline of Shanghai as being among the world's best skylines and ranked Hong Kong as being "the most beautiful in the world, hands down". When you consider that there are so many ways to experience and enjoy the skyline of Chinese cities like Hong Kong and the fact that the nation boasts a rare combination of man-made and natural beauty and ancient architecture meshed with modern architecture, you can't help but understand why photographing China's major cities was a complete joy.

Without question, there has been a major building boom and a great transformation in the overall look of the major cities in China because of the increase in construction over the past decade. It has been fascinating to watch the development and evolution of the skylines and changes in architecture of cities like Beijing, Shanghai and Hangzhou. In recent years, the World Bank predicted that by 2015, half of the world's new building construction will take place in China, which means that the look of these Chinese cities, along with many others, will continue to transform, making for an exciting new urban landscape for the world to enjoy.

Photographer's Impressions:

As I traveled around China and marveled at the creative and innovative architectural design of the buildings, both modern and traditional, from Beijing, Shanghai, Hong Kong, Xi'an, Dunhuang, Changsha and Lanzhou and all places in between, the value of preserving the old with the integration of the new can be seen throughout the country. Many foreigners who have never visited China would be totally amazed and impressed with the architectural diversity and magnificence found in this great country. (The design and construction of the "Bird's Nest" for the Olympics and the design and construction of the China Pavilion for the 2010 Shanghai World Expo are examples of modern Chinese architectural brilliance.)

One of the unexpected delights that I discovered early in my travels throughout China is that good shots were not limited to the daylight hours. Night time provides an entirely different look at the same cities and skylines. I found it very interesting that the Chinese government and people take conservation of energy very seriously, and lights and other energy consuming items such as air-conditioners and heating units are on timers, which control and monitor usage. However, when it comes to lighting up the cities and towns at night, conservation takes a "back seat" to beautifying the cities. In my opinion, no other country in the world comes close to presenting its cities with the kind of flare and multi-colored brilliance as China at night. It is like celebrating an "American Christmas" every night in China.

一个人要想真正了解当代中国，就必须懂得欣赏中国现代建筑与天际线的美丽及宏伟。近年来，TravelersDigest.com网站将上海的天际线列为世界上最具"未来主义"的天际线，而将香港的天际线评为"世界上最美丽的天际线"。中国有如此之多的优美天际线——如香港的天际线——可供体验与享受，拥有人为景观与自然风光、古代建筑与现代建筑的完美组合，因此拍摄中国的主要城市实在是一件赏心悦目的乐事。

毫无疑问，过去十年，中国主要城市都掀起一股建设热潮，各大城市建筑的整体外观发生了翻天覆地的变化。北京、上海和杭州等城市不断高耸的天际线和持续变化的建筑物让人啧啧称奇。近年来，世界银行预测，到2015年，世界上新开工的建筑有一半在中国。这意味着，中国城市的面貌将会持续发生改变，向世界呈现一幅激动人心的新城市景观。

感言：

走在中国的大街小巷，我每每感叹于中国古代建筑与现代建筑构思的精巧与新颖。不论是在北京、上海、香港、西安、敦煌、长沙、兰州还是在中国其他地方，中国古建筑与现代建筑交相辉映，相映成趣。从未访问过中国的外国人将诧异于这个伟大国度建筑物的千姿百态与宏伟壮观。奥运场馆"鸟巢"以及2010上海世博会中国馆的设计与施工堪称现代中国建筑的典范，充分展示了中国人民的聪明才智。

刚到中国时，我惊喜地发现：要拍摄佳作并不仅限于白天。夜幕赋予同一座城市及其天际线一张截然不同的面孔。有意思的是，中国政府和人民非常重视节能，灯光及其他用电设施，如：空调和取暖设备都安装有定时器，负责监控其使用。但是，每当夜幕降临，城市"亮化工程"就让节能用电坐上了"冷板凳"，中国城镇呈现出灯火辉煌、五光十色的另一番景象。在中国，每个夜晚都像在庆祝"美国圣诞节"。

Skyscrapers and construction sites in Shanghai. This photo is reflective of the explosive economic growth in China.

上海的摩天大楼和建筑工地。这张照片反映出中国经济的迅猛增长。

An important historical site. It is the location of the first session of the Communist party in China. Shanghai, China.
中共一大会址，是中国上海一处重要的历史遗址。

Photo of the world class city of Hong Kong, a modern cosmopolitan city.
香港，一座现代化的国际大都会。

Ancient cultural street near Tianjin outside of Beijing.
中国天津古文化街。

The Mother Yellow River—Lanzhou. The river runs through the City of Lanzhou and plays a vital role in commerce and trade in China. It is the second longest river in China next to the Yangtze River. It is known by many as the "cradle of Chinese civilization".

黄河——中国的母亲河，摄于兰州。黄河贯穿整个兰州市，对中国商贸起着至关重要的作用。黄河是中国第二长的河流，仅次于长江。中国人祝黄河为"中华文明的摇篮"。

Night scene of the Aiwan Pavilion located in Changsha, Hunan Province. Many local Chinese gather around the Pavilion during the evening and night to enjoy the summer nights after long scorching days in Changsha.

湖南长沙爱晚亭夜景。夜晚，经过白天烈日的炙烤，许多长沙当地人会聚集在亭子四周，享受漫漫夏夜。

A pavilion near the old Walls of Xi'an.
西安古城墙附近的亭子。

Shanghai at night
上海夜景

The Bund area of Shanghai at night. It is one of the most popular tourist attraction of the city. It "lights up like a Christmas tree at night". In this area of Shanghai, one can spot many locals and foreigners who hang out to eat, shop, and be entertained.

上海外滩万国建筑群夜景。上海外滩是上海最热门的旅游景点之一，每当夜幕降临,外滩处处灯火辉煌、流光溢彩。在这儿，你不难发现许多当地人和外国人结伴下馆子、购物和开展各项娱乐活动。

Shanghai on National Day night in 2010
上海，摄于2010年国庆之夜

FRIENDSHIP
友谊

My ability to tell the photographic story that appears within these pages would have been greatly diminished were it not for the many friendships that I have established with people throughout my travels in China. Friendship and the idea of brotherhood mean a lot to the Chinese people, and I wanted to reflect those cultural values in my work. Without the relationships that I have been able to establish during my visit to China, my photographs would have felt much like those of an average tourist who goes about clicking shots of strange people and places that they are likely to never see again. On most of my journeys, I have had the benefit of traveling with individuals who had a keen knowledge of the history of a location or intimate stories of their experiences there. These insights guided my work and allowed me to look more intimately into the true story behind every location and every face. There is a tremendous amount of satisfaction in capturing an image which carries with it a sort of intimacy with which not everyone is familiar.

Photographer's Impressions:

There are simply no words to describe the many friendships that I have developed throughout the years during my travels to China. I have been fortunate to have met and made friends at all levels of the Chinese society. I will cherish these associations for the rest of my life. In fact, this book will serve as a lasting reminder to me of a decade of good times and good friends, with fond thoughts of continuing old friendships and building new ones in the years ahead.

若非在中国旅行期间我与中国人民建立起的深厚友谊，本书所要讲述的图片背后的故事将大打折扣。中国人民十分看重友谊和兄弟情谊，我想通过图片展现中国人民的这种文化价值观。如果不是因为我与中国人民建立起的深厚友谊，我拍摄的照片与寻常游客拍摄的照片将别无二致，不过是每到一地，按下快门，拍下那些陌生的人与物，之后再也不会看它们一眼。我在中国旅行期间常得益于当地那些对风景了如指掌的人，他们熟知当地景点的历史与逸事。这些丰富生动的描述引领我深入探寻每一处风景、每一张面孔背后真实的故事。因此，能够拍摄一张于他人熟视无睹，于己却蕴涵丰富的图像真是人生一大快事。

感言：

很难用合适的词来形容这些年我在中国旅行期间与当地人建立起来的友谊。我庆幸自己能结识中国社会各阶层的人并与他们成为朋友。在我的余生，我会加倍珍惜这份情谊。事实上，这本书会时刻提醒我在过往十年里在中国度过的美好时光，勾起我对好友的回忆。在今后的岁月里，我将结识新朋友，不忘老朋友。

The Chairman of the University Council greeting Elizabeth McPhee , my wife, at his office at China Agricultural University in Beijing. Generally, Chinese people are not known for displaying emotions in public as seen in this photo. The Chairman and the McPhees have become very close personal friends over the years as he has visited my university in Tennessee, USA and has been a guest in our home during his stay in the United States. For these reasons, this is one of my favorite photos.

北京中国农业大学校理事会主席在办公室会见我的我妻子伊丽莎白·麦克菲。一般来说，中国人在公共场合不会像照片上那样将感情轻易外露。中国农大校理事会主席到美国中田纳西州州立大学参观访问期间与我们一家人建立了深厚的友谊，是我们家的座上宾。正因如此，这张照片成为我最喜欢的照片之一。

A Chinese boy at the Garden in Suzhou.
中国男孩，摄于苏州园林。

Photographer and Tang Jianwen (Martin), Director, Office of International Exchange and Cooperation at Hunan Normal University.
与湖南师范大学国际交流合作处处长唐建文合影。

Being invited to the home of a Chinese family is the ultimate honor and sign of true friendship. The photo was taken in the home of a local Chinese family who lived in Haining near Hangzhou, China.
被邀请到中国人家里做客是无上的光荣，也象征着纯真友谊。

Planting a friendship tree at Central South University of Forestry and Technology in Changsha.
种植友谊树，于长沙中南林业科技大学。

Special Chinese friends from Schenzhen (mother and daughter) who accompanied me to Hong Kong and helped me with my re-entry Visa problem.
特别的中国朋友。这对深圳母女陪同我赴港并帮我解决了再次入关的签证问题。

This photo was taken during a train ride to Hong Kong from Shenzhen. I was accompanied by a Chinese family (mother and daughter) that I was introduced to by a mutual Chinese friend and colleague who served as Vice President at China Agricultural University in Beijing. The mother and the CAU Vice President were former classmates in high school from Inner Mongolia Autonomous Region. The mother and daughter showed me a wonderful time in Hong Kong. Upon our return to Shenzhen, I was stopped at the border checkpoint by a Chinese immigration officer who told me in "Chinglish", "No visa". I politely and nervously responded, "I do have a visa" and pointed to the page in the passport. But, he said in a more firm tone, "No visa" and brushed me aside. By this time, my hosts who were standing in the Chinese resident re-entry line had already crossed over on the other side of the checkpoint. For me, the panic began to set in. The Chinese immigration officer went over and told my hosts that I was not going to be allowed to re-enter because my visa had expired. Luckily for me, I was with some very caring and concerned Chinese friends who returned on the other side of the checkpoint to help me out of my situation. It was explained to me that my original Chinese visa was a single entry visa and once I left Shenzhen for my brief visit to Hong Kong, my visa had expired.

I needed a new visa to re-enter mainland China. I was not going to be allowed to go back to Shenzhen without a new visa, which meant that I had to go back to the downtown Hong Kong area to the Chinese Embassy office and apply for a new visa. I had to get a passport picture, complete an application and wait for the visa to be processed and approved. My hosts accompanied me to get a passport picture, assisted me in completing the application and through some persuasion, in Chinese of course, with the Chinese Embassy officials, I was able to secure a new Chinese visa by late afternoon that same day, just in time to catch the last train back to Shenzhen. I would have been "up the creek without a paddle" had it not for the kindness of my friends from Shenzhen. The lesson learned, always apply for a multiple-entry visa when visiting China.

　　这张照片拍摄于从深圳前往香港的火车上。一位在北京中国农业大学担任副校长的中国友人兼同事介绍一对中国母女陪我前往香港。这位母亲与中国农业大学副校长是高中同学，原就读于内蒙古自治区。母女二人带我游览香港，陪我度过了一段美好时光。返回深圳时，我在过关时被中国边检站的一位入境检查人员拦住，他用中式英语对我说："没签证。"我礼貌而又紧张地回答道"我有签证"，并指向护照上相应的页面。但是，他用更严厉的语气说"没签证"并把我晾到一边。这时，排在中国居民再入境线另一侧的母女俩已过关，到了边检站的另一边。我开始感到一阵恐慌。中国入境检查人员走过去，告诉母女二人我不能重新入境，因为我的签证已过期。幸运的是，母女二人非常体贴，她们重新回到边检站的这一侧，帮我脱离窘境。我这才明白我的中国原始签证是单次入境签证，一旦我离开深圳对香港做短暂访问，我的签证就已经过期。

　　我需要申请新的签证才能重返中国大陆。没有新签证，我将不能返回深圳，这也意味着我必须到位于香港市中心的中国大使馆申请新的签证。我必须拿到一张护照照片，填写一份申请表，等待申请审核通过并签发新的签证。陪我一同来港的母女俩耐心地陪我领取护照照片、协助我填写申请表，并用中文与中国大使馆官员交涉，使我得以在当天傍晚拿到新的中国签证，及时赶上回深圳的末班火车。如果没有朋友们的鼎力相助，我将深陷困境。这以后，我吸取此次出行的教训，再次出访中国时都申请多次入境签证。

Photo of graduates of Central South University of Forestry and Technology in Changsha and the President of the University.
长沙中南林业科技大学的毕业生与校长。

Enjoying a good time with friends from China South Publishing & Media Group in Changsha,China
与中南出版传媒集团的朋友们合影，摄于长沙。

My "big brother" Vice Governor Zhangliang Chen of the Guangxi Zhuang Autonomous Region. He likes to tell me that we are from the same mother but "a different color."

我"大哥"广西壮族自治区副省长陈章良。他常说我们同源只是母亲皮肤的颜色不一样罢了。

Meeting with one of the youngest living Buddha in the Monastery in Xining. We had a wonderful conversation. He asked me about my family and blessed me and gave me a hada.

与西宁寺年轻的活佛会面。我们交谈甚欢，他仔细询问我的家人，向我献上祝福，并赠予我一条哈达。

Demonstration to the Chinese chef at the hotel restaurant how to prepare an American omelet for breakfast. The next year while staying at this same hotel in Lanzhou, the chef brought me an omelet to my table without me ordering it. It was well prepared like an American breakfast.

向酒店餐厅的中国厨师示范如何准备美国人早餐常吃的美式煎蛋。第二年，我入住兰州同一家酒店，尽管我未点煎蛋，厨师仍给我端上一份美式煎蛋。蛋煎得很棒，完全可与美式早餐媲美。

Newly made friends who were working in the Yellow Mountain.
在黄山工作的新朋友。

Terra Cotta Warriors Museum with Wang Limin in Xi'an.
与王利民摄于西安兵马俑博物馆。

Hanging out with two beautiful Chinese girls in Suzhou, China.
与两名靓丽的中国女孩合影留念，摄于苏州。

Enjoying some good time with two young Chinese boys in Lanzhou, China.
与两位中国小男孩合影留念，摄于兰州。

A village near the Tian Ti Shan Buddha site in Wuwei, Gansu. The youngest child in the photo approached me and gave me a crumpled piece of paper and the words written in English said "Welcome to China. I love you."

甘肃武威天梯山石窟附近的一个村庄。照片中最小的孩子走到我面前，递给我一张皱巴巴的纸，上面用英语写着："欢迎来到中国，我爱你。"

Zhouzhuang, China
摄于中国周庄。

A local Chinese enjoying a Chinese dinner in the Yellow Mountain area. Note the many varieties of dishes served during the first course.

一名中国本地人在黄山景区享用中式晚餐。需要注意的是：中餐第一轮上菜时会同时呈上多种菜肴。

CHINESE CUISINE AND DINING
中国美食与烹调

When it comes to Chinese food, many Americans will declare, with great confidence, that they are quite knowledgeable about Chinese cuisine...that is until they actually visit China and see that many popular dishes created to suit Western tastes aren't readily available or that authentic Chinese meals differ greatly when prepared in Eastern cultures. As with other nations, food is an important part of the Chinese culture, but what makes it different is the great symbolism that is attached to eating and drinking in China. Everything from the food that is served to where people sit has an important meaning.

When you are traveling in China, you quickly come to understand that eating is about more than simply relieving hunger. Dining is an experience in beauty, balance and harmony, and having an abundance of food signifies happiness, good fortune and good health. When it comes to both main dishes and the food items that accompany them, there is usually great variety. And how food is presented in terms of its plating is just as important as the food itself because each dish is its own work of art, meant to appeal to all of one's senses.

Another special aspect of dining in the Chinese culture is the interaction among people. The dining experience is joyful and lively and is designed to bring people closer together. The tradition of toasting is one of the aspects of the Chinese meal that makes dining in this country such a dynamic experience. Unlike in America, where you might expect a single toast during a meal, there are generally several toasts, usually with shots of "Maotai", a very strong liquor, which registers in at about 120 proof. These toasts traditionally conclude with the word "Gan bei!" which basically means "bottoms up". These toasting rituals are designed to show respect and friendship and to build and strengthen relationships among those present.

Photographer's Impressions:

As a self-proclaimed connoisseur of food and drink, I frequently announce China as one of my favorite countries in which to dine. Every region has its own unique style or tradition of cuisine, with Cantonese being among my favorites. I have enjoyed everything from what would be considered traditional, everyday Chinese meals with friends to elaborate banquets that were seemingly fit for royalty. I have never left a Chinese table without feeling more energized and closer to my host and dinner companions, including those who may have been traveling with me. I enjoy sharing the photographs of my dining experiences in China because each meal comes with its own unique and exciting story about beautifully prepared food and wonderful people. The stories get even livelier with each dinner toast that I recall.

提到中华美食，许多美国人不无自信地宣称他们对中国菜了如指掌、如数家珍。但是，如果他们来过中国，亲自品尝过中华美食，也许就不会这么自得了。在中国，那些为了适应西方人的口味而量身打造的中国菜已难觅踪迹，正宗的中国菜与西方中餐馆里的中国菜有着天壤之别。和其他国家一样，饮食是中国文化不可或缺的一部分，而中国人赋予"吃""喝"的深厚意蕴又使它有别于他国的饮食文化。呈上餐桌的每一道菜肴都有着非同一般的意义。

在中国旅游，你很快就会意识到，吃不仅仅是裹腹而已。用餐是一种融美丽、均衡与和谐于一体的感官享受，与此同时，丰盛的食品也是幸福、吉祥与健康的象征。中华美食由主菜与配菜构成，品种繁多、各具特色。此外，中国菜的装盘与食物本身一样考究，因为每道菜都是一件精美的艺术品，每一道色、香、味、形俱全的菜肴都能带给就餐者感官上的完美享受。

中国餐饮文化的一大特色就是用餐过程中人与人之间的互动，整个就餐过程气氛愉悦、热闹，有利于增进人与人之间的情谊。中国人吃饭时会敬酒，敬酒使得吃饭不再是一个静态的过程，而是一次动态的体验。在美国，席间会致一次祝酒辞，但是，在中国，一餐饭下来往往要敬几个回合的酒，酒桌上常喝到"茅台"。"茅台"酒劲很大，一般在50度左右。祝酒结束时人们通常会说"干杯！"。这些祝酒仪式不仅仅是对就餐者的尊重，也有利于建立和增强彼此之间的情谊。

感言：

我常自诩为美食与美酒行家，谈到美食，我常跟人说，中国是我最喜欢的国度之一。在中国，各个地区的饮食都有着自己的独特风味或传统，其中，粤菜是我的最爱。我喜欢与三两好友小酌时的传统家常小菜，也享受丰盛的"皇家"宴席。每次就餐结束，我都感到精神焕发，与主人、同伴以及那些陪同我旅游的人的关系也更为紧密。我乐于分享我在中国就餐时的照片，因为每次就餐都有着精心准备的别具一格的食品以及来自不同地区却同样热情好客的朋友。每每回想起这些人与事，我记忆深处那一幅幅祝酒的画面就变得鲜活起来。

Mongolian beef served at a local Mongolian restaurant in Shenzhen
在深圳当地一家蒙古餐厅分享蒙古牛肉

Chinese tea break at the minorities' villages in Yunnan Province. China is known for its green tea.
云南省少数民族村落里的中国茶歇。中国绿茶驰名天下。

A beautifully presented fruit dish with apples and watermelon. Watermelon is very popular in China. It is served at the end of most dinners as the dessert.
用苹果与西瓜做成的精美的水果拼盘。西瓜在中国很受大众欢迎，常用做餐后甜点。

Squirrel fish. This is my very favorite Chinese dish. I always order this dish if available when I am in China. I highly recommend it.
松鼠鳜鱼——我最喜欢的一道中国菜。在中国时，只要餐馆里可以供应松鼠鳜鱼，我都会点上这道菜。我强烈向各位读者推荐这道菜。

A chef preparing Shanxi noodles in Xi'an
陕西西安，一名厨师正在做面条

Chinese vegetables. A Chinese dinner is incomplete without an array of vegetable dishes to sample. It is a very healthy part of the Chinese diet.
中国蔬菜。在中国，一餐饭下来，如果没有蔬菜助阵就不算一顿完美的中餐。荤素搭配是中国人健康饮食的一部分。

An exquisite private dining room in a beautifully decorated restaurant in Beijing. Unlike most American restaurants, most Chinese restaurants have private dining rooms that are elaborately decorated and provide privacy for guests when dining.
雅致的包厢，摄于北京一家装修华丽的餐馆。与大多数美国餐馆不同的是，大多数中国餐馆都有装潢考究的包厢以保护客人就餐时的隐私。

CHINA ON THE
WORLD STAGE:
BEIJING 2008
OLYMPICS & 2010
WORLD EXPO
登上世界舞台
的中国：北京
2008奥运会及
2010世博会

China's leaders have come to realize that, like other major powers, the country needs to get its own message out to secure its share of good press and positive perceptions. And China has a lot to offer in this area.
———The Straits Times (Feb. 12, 2011)

China's hosting of the 2008 Summer Olympics in Beijing was viewed by many as a "coming-of-age event" for China, representing to the world its "rise as a new global power, backed by a dynamic national economy…" In a similar manner, its hosting of the 2010 World Expo, featuring fantastically designed pavilions developed by countries from around the world, is also said to have represented a turning point for the Country. In both of these recent instances, most people would agree that China succeeded in its attempts to gain recognition on the world stage, and its efforts were highly chronicled in various media for the entire world to see. As recorded in a *Washington Post* news article at the end of the event, "hosting the Olympics was good for the world and for China." It was noted that the Summer Olympics helped to "bring the country (China) into the fold of the international community" and that many of those who wouldn't have previously considered coming to China visited because of the games. According to Nielsen Media Research, 4.7 billion viewers worldwide tuned in to some of the television coverage of the summer Olympics that year. Likewise, the 2010 World Expo attracted a record-setting crowd of more than 70 million visitors and some 246 countries and international organizations.

Photographer's Impressions:

The photos in this section show the creativity, ingenuity, and brilliance of the Chinese people. China exploded on the world stage in a major way with its successful production and delivery of the 2008 Beijing Olympics, followed by the 2010 Shanghai World Expo. It was exciting to see the transformation of these two major cities as they prepared to showcase China to the world. I was privileged to have had the opportunity to attend both of these historic and exciting worldwide events and to document various aspects of them on camera. Other nations will find great difficulty in matching China's success in hosting these two events in the future.

中国领导人已经意识到，应像其他世界强国一样在世界舞台上发出自己的声音，以获得外媒良好的新闻形象和广泛的认同。中国为此做出了许多努力。——《海峡时报》（2011年2月12日）

中国成功举办的2008北京夏季奥运会被许多人看做是中国的"成人礼"，它向全世界宣称"以生机勃勃的国民经济为坚强后盾的中国已经迅速崛起，成为新的世界强国。"与之类似，中国还成功主办了2010年世博会，世界各国设计的各具特色的展馆为世博会积聚了大量人气，被视为中国的一个重要转折点。不可否认，这两项盛事表明中国已经成功获得世界的认同，其努力已见诸于世界各大媒体。2008北京奥运会之后，《华盛顿邮报》发表新闻文章称"举办奥运会既有利于世界，也有利于中国"。"文中特别提到"，2008夏季奥运会成功地"将中国纳入国际社会"，在此之前许多没有打算来中国旅游的人如潮水般涌入中国。尼尔森媒介研究称，全球共有47亿观众通过电视收看北京奥运会。同样，2010年世博会吸引了创纪录的超过7000万游客和246个国家及国际组织参展。

感言：

本章照片充分展示了中国人民的卓越创造，精湛手工和聪明才智。中国先后成功承办了2008北京奥运会和2010上海世博会，震撼了世界舞台。能亲眼目睹这两座城市为向世界更好地展现中国而做出的巨大改变着实令人兴奋。我有幸参与这两项具有重大历史意义的、激动人心的、引起全世界关注的盛事，并用手中的相机记录下这两项盛事的多个画面。未来，其他国家要想在这两项事件上超越中国真比登天还难。

The "Bird Nest", one of the many architecturally innovative sport venues constructed in Beijing for the 2008 Olympics. This photo was taken on the evening that Jamaican track star Usain Bolt broke the world record in the 100 meter track race. I witnessed this historic event with my wife, son, and daughter. It was one of the most electrifying sporting events I have ever seen.

"鸟巢"，北京2008年奥运会众多匠心独具的体育场馆之一。这张照片摄于牙买加田径明星博尔特打破100米世界纪录当晚。我、我妻子、我儿子与女儿亲眼目睹了这一历史性事件，这是我见过的最激动人心的体育赛事之一。

Inside the Bird Nest during a track and field Olympic event. It was a magical and historic evening.
奥运会田径赛期间摄于鸟巢内部。这是一个奇妙的、具有历史意义的夜晚。

A photo with Renjie Dong, the Director of China Agricultural University Affairs Office of International Affairs, at a wrestling Olympic match hosted by the university.

与中国农业大学国际合作与交流处处长董仁杰在奥运会摔跤场馆合影。中国农业大学承办了2008年奥运会的摔跤比赛项目。

The beautifully designed and constructed Chinese pavilion at the 2010 Shanghai World Expo.
设计精美、结构精巧的中国馆，摄于2010年上海世博会。

The Urban Pavilion at the Shanghai 2010 World Expo. My wife, daughter, the Odens—our friends, along with Chinese visitors at the Expo.
2010年上海世博会城市馆。我妻子、女儿与我们的朋友奥登一家与中国游客在世博会合影留念。

2010 Shanghai World Expo lit up at night. Brilliant designs and colors.
2010年上海世博会夜晚亮灯时的场景。设计精妙，色彩斑斓。

The photo insert was taken of a cultural show "Impressions of the West Lake" in Hangzhou, China.
插入的图片为中国杭州"西湖印象"文化演出的照片。

Inside bridge in the Chinese Pavilion. Bridge to the future and cultures.
中国馆内部的一座小桥，通往未来与文化之桥。

Exhibition of the growing of rice as displayed in the Chinese Pavilion at the Shanghai World Expo. It demonstrates the importance of rice for the Chinese people.

上海世博会中国馆的水稻栽培展览，表明水稻对中国人民生活的重要性。

Digital photo display of the Temple of Heaven in the Chinese Pavilion.

中国馆用数码图片呈现的天坛。

图书在版编目（CIP）数据

一位美国校长眼中的中国 / （美）麦克菲著；张晓舸
译.—长沙：湖南美术出版社，2012.5
ISBN 978-7-5356-5402-1

Ⅰ.①一… Ⅱ.①麦…②张… Ⅲ.①中国–概况–摄
影集 Ⅳ.①K92–64

中国版本图书馆CIP数据核字(2012)第092963号

一位美国校长
眼中的中国

China Through The Eyes of
An American University President

Publisher: Li Xiaoshan	出 版 人：李小山
Supervisor: Zhang Xiao, Yan Hua	监 制：张 晓 颜 华
Planner: Zheng Guanping	策 划：郑冠平
Author: Sidney A.McPhee(U.S.A)	著 者：西德尼·A·麦克菲
Translator: Zhang Xiaoge	翻 译：张晓舸
Editor in charge: Liu Yingzheng, Liu Haizhen, Zheng Liang	责任编辑：刘迎蒸 刘海珍 郑 良
Cover Designer: Dai Yu	装帧设计：戴 宇
	责任校对：彭 慧
Publishing and distribution house: Hunan Fine Arts Publishing House (No 622, Section 1, Eastern Beltway 2, Changsha, Hunan, China)	出版发行：湖南美术出版社 （长沙市东二环一段622号）
Distributor: Hunan Xinhua Bookstore Co., Ltd.	经 销：湖南省新华书店
Plate-making: JARL.V CULTURE	制 版：嘉伟文化 JARL.V CULTURE
Printing House: Everbest Printing(Guangzhou)Co Ltd (334 Huanshi Road South,Nansha,Guangdong,China)	印 刷：恒美印务（广州）有限公司 （广州市南沙开发区环市大道南334号）
Size: 889 × 1194 1/16	开 本：889×1194 1/16
Sheets: 9	印 张：9
Version: June 2012, first edition; June 2012, first printing	版 次：2012年6月第1版 2012年6月第1次印刷
ISBN: ISBN 978-7-5356-5402-1	书 号：ISBN 978-7-5356-5402-1
Price: CNY ¥78.00 / USD $29.95	定 价：¥78.00元 / $29.95美元